Christmas *in* Italy *and* Vatican City

A Christmas
display in
Milan.

Christmas *in* Italy *and* Vatican City

Christmas Around the World
from World Book

World Book, Inc.
a Scott Fetzer company
Chicago

Staff

Editorial

Editor-in-Chief
Paul A. Kobasa

Executive Editor
Sara Dreyfuss

Managing Editor
Maureen Mostyn Liebenson

Editor
Christine Sullivan

Assistant Editor
Lisa Kwon

Permissions Editor
Janet T. Peterson

Cartography

Manager, Digital Cartography
Wayne K. Pichler

Research

Manager, Research Services
Loranne K. Shields

Senior Researcher
Lynn Durbin

Art

Manager, Graphics and Design
Sandra Dyrlund

Senior Designer
Don Di Sante

Photographs Editor
Kathy Creech

*Production and Administrative
Support*
John Whitney

Production

*Director, Manufacturing and
Pre-Press*
Carma Fazio

Manager, Manufacturing
Barbara Podczerwinski

Senior Production Manager
Madelyn Underwood

Production Manager
Anne Fritzinger

Print Promotional Manager
Marco Morales

Proofreader
Anne Dillon

Text Processing
Gwendolyn Johnson

Marketing

Director, Direct Marketing
Mark R. Willy

Marketing Analyst
Zofia Kulik

World Book, Inc.
233 N. Michigan Ave.
Chicago, IL 60601

For information about other World Book publications, visit our Web site at **www.worldbook.com** or call **1-800-WORLDBK (967-5325)**. For information about sales to schools and libraries, call **1-800-975-3250 (United States)**, or **1-800-837-5365 (Canada)**.

Library of Congress Cataloging-in-Publication Data

Christmas in Italy and Vatican City.
   p. cm. -- (Christmas around the world from World Book)
  ISBN 0-7166-0805-7
  1. Christmas--Italy. 2. Christmas--Vatican City. 3. Italy--Social life and customs. 4. Vatican City--Social life and customs. I.World Book, Inc. II. Series.
  GT4987.51.C37 2006
  394.2663'0945--dc22

                 2005016630

Printed in the United States of America
1 2 3 4 5 10 09 08 07 06 05

Contents

Traditions

Christmas really began in Italy. Christ was born in the tiny village of Bethlehem, in the ancient Middle Eastern kingdom of Judea. But His birth was first celebrated in Rome almost 300 years later, after the Emperor Constantine adopted the new faith of Christianity.

Church leaders in those times often substituted saints for pagan gods and Christian holy days for pagan celebrations. No one knows for certain, even today, the exact date of Christ's birth. The feast day of the Roman's old pagan god Mithra, however, fell on December 25, and that was the day chosen to honor Christ.

The period between mid-December and early January had long been one of almost nonstop revelry in ancient Rome. It began with the Saturnalia, a winter solstice festival, and ended with the Roman New Year, the Festival of the Calends. It was a joyous time of good will and sharing. People exchanged visits and gave gifts, especially at New Year's Day. Candles and clay dolls were favorite presents; dates, figs, honey, and coins were also popular. Laurel branches were given as gifts, too—these branches were used to decorate houses and temples.

The Tuscan town of Sansepolcro, lighted for Christmas.

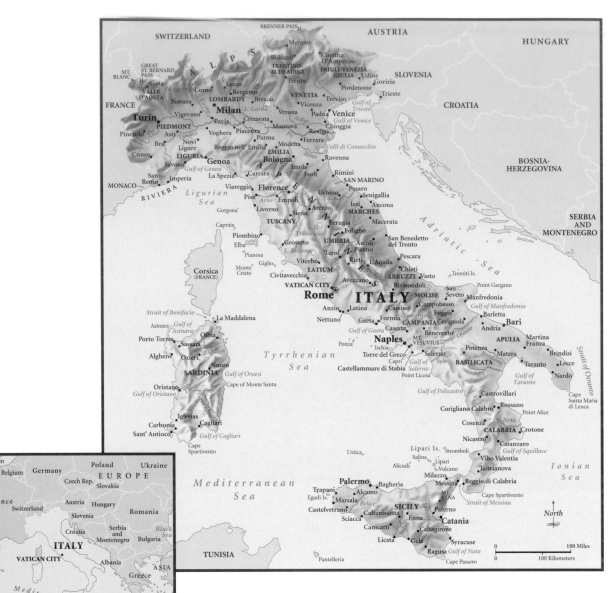

A map of Italy (above right) *and a map of Europe* (inset).

After the coming of Christianity, the season became a time of holiness, of reverence for Christ. Instead of ending at New Year's Day, it extended to January 6, the Feast of the Epiphany, when the Church celebrated the arrival of the Three Kings in Bethlehem. The Kings gave their gifts to the infant Jesus on that day, and so the Romans, too, began to exchange presents on Epiphany.

Christmas in Italy today is still very much a religious holiday. The season begins with a Christmas *novena* (a word that comes from the Latin *novem*, meaning nine). This is a nine-day period of special church services ending on Christmas Eve.

While many Christmas trees may be seen nowadays in Italy, the real focal point of Christmas observances is the Nativity scene. These

Nativity scenes range from simple, homemade re-creations of the old Bible story to elaborate displays containing hundreds of pieces and dozens of different scenes. The image of the Christ child in His crib is deeply cherished by Italians and the country is overflowing with Nativity scenes at Christmastime. Presents are often placed near the manger, and families pray together in front of it.

Important as religion is to most Italians, however, the Christmas season is not devoted only to churchgoing and prayer. Children put on plays in school, give recitations, and make decorations. Families make special trips to the colorful Christmas markets to buy presents and new manger figures. Window-shopping is great fun—stores and streets are all gaily decorated with lights and Christmas greenery.

The opera season opens in December, too, and nowadays those who can afford it often go on ski vacations. In Sicily, puppet shows are a holiday tradition, with large, hand-carved puppets acting out fairy tales and legendary battles.

Christmas Eve and Christmas Day are strictly family affairs. There's an old saying that goes: "You can spend New Year's with anyone you choose, but Christmas is for family." December 26, St. Stephen's Day,

Children singing Christmas carols at a school party in Milan (above) *and the flag of Italy* (below). *Italy's tricolor flag of green, white, and red dates to the late 1700's.*

A life-sized Nativity scene displayed in St. Peter's Square, in Vatican City. To the right of the manger display is the Vatican Christmas tree, while an obelisk from ancient Egypt and St. Peter's Basilica can be seen behind the stable in the background.

was once a day of religious devotion. Now, it is mostly one of rest or visiting. People call on friends and relatives, bringing gifts and sharing holiday foods. And they go to see some of the many marvelous manger displays.

New Year's Eve is celebrated with parties, dancing, champagne, and fireworks. Shortly after New Year's, children return to school, but the end of the Christmas season does not actually come until Epiphany.

Christmas in Italy is religious in character, but Christmas in Vatican City, as might be expected, is even more so. Vatican City, the smallest independent nation in the world, is the spiritual and governmental center of the Roman Catholic Church.

The Vatican's holiday season begins with Advent—which begins about four Sundays before Christmas Day and ends on Christmas Eve. Advent is the beginning of the Church's liturgical year and serves in

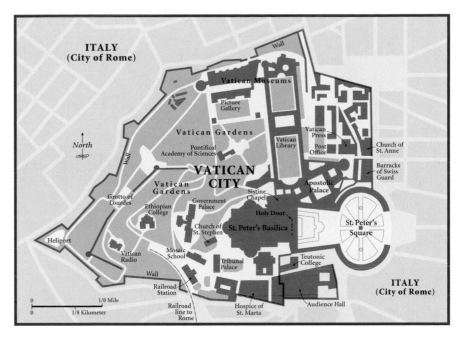

A map and the national flag of Vatican City. The emblem on the flag's white stripe is the Vatican's coat of arms— a papal tiara above crossed keys.

Roman Catholicism as a time of spiritual preparation for Christmas. At some point during Advent, a life-sized Nativity scene is placed in St. Peter's Square. With the arrival of a Polish pope in 1978— Karol Wojtyla, who became John Paul II (1920–2005)—the custom of the Christmas tree was eventually introduced to the Vatican, as well. The Vatican tree is donated each year from a different region of Europe and stands some 100 feet high in St. Peter's Square.

Thousands of visitors come to Vatican City to see the Christmas Masses. On Christmas Eve, the pope celebrates Mass in St. Peter's Basilica. The pontiff also presides at the Christmas Day Mass, which is usually offered in St. Peter's Square, just outside the Basilica. After the Christmas Mass, he gives an address called Urbi et Orbi (To the City [of Rome] and the World), traditionally from the balcony of the Basilica. He also blesses the visitors who assemble in the Square.

The Christmas season continues for the Vatican with the Feast of the Epiphany on January 6. From the Greek word that means "to appear or show one's self," Epiphany celebrates the time when tradition claims the world (the Three Magi, or Kings) first saw Christ. The Vatican's holiday celebrations close on the Sunday after Epiphany with a mass that honors Jesus's baptism.

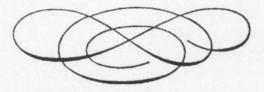

Celebrations

Italy is a land of diverse regions; a narrow country shaped some-
what like a boot. It stretches almost 1,000 miles, from the snow-
covered Alps to sun-baked Sicily. Actually, Sicily is an island; on
a map, it looks something like the ball that the boot is about to
kick. Sardinia, another island of Italy, lies northwest of Sicily,
about 135 miles west of Rome.

In the mountain provinces of Italy, Christmases are cold, with lots
of ice and snow. In Rome, the holidays may be touched with a hint
of springlike weather. Most likely, it will be chilly and damp. In the
south, midwinter days are usually warm and sunny.

Christmas customs are just as varied as the weather; even within a
particular region they are not always the same. Exchanging gifts, for
instance, occurs on a whole raft of different days.

On December 6, the feast day of San Nicola (Saint Nicholas), the
saint is said to visit many of the children of Bari and other towns along
the Adriatic coast. Nicholas was archbishop of Myra in Asia Minor in
the mid-300's. Legend says that his remains were stolen in 1087 by a
band of Italian clergy and merchants. They carried them to Bari, in the

On a canal in Venice, a Christmas tree is delivered by boat.

region of Apulia, Italy, and there a shrine was built in Nicholas's honor. A festival is held each year on his feast day, and thousands of people make pilgrimages to his tomb.

In Sicily, Santa Lucia (Saint Lucy) brings presents on her feast day, December 13. Like Saint Nicholas, Lucy lived in the 300's. She was condemned to death, some say because she refused the attentions of a wicked nobleman. Others believe it was because she defended her unpopular beliefs. St. Lucy, accompanied by a donkey carrying baskets of gifts, goes about her rounds wearing a blue, star-sprinkled cloak. Youngsters place their shoes outside the door the night before, hoping to find them filled with presents in the morning. Boys and girls sometimes place food outdoors, too—for the donkey.

Way up in the snowy north of Italy, in Cortina D'Ampezzo, a spectacular event is held on Christmas Eve. It is called the Fiaccolate degli Sciatori. At midnight, the Alpine guides, holding flaming torches, ski down the mountainside. Darting over the slopes in sweeping curves and crisscross patterns, the skiers look like a giant cloud of fireflies flashing across the night.

Italy is a vibrant, exciting place to be at Christmastime. In Rome, at sunset on Christmas Eve, cannons boom from the Castel Sant' Angelo (Castle of St. Angelo), announcing the start of the holy season. A few hours later, the city's streets are jammed with crowds heading for one of its more than 400 churches. Nearby, in Vatican City, the pope himself conducts the Midnight Mass at St. Peter's. Vatican City is the smallest country in the world. It is completely surrounded by Rome and is ruled by the pope, the leader of the Roman Catholic Church.

The custom of exchanging gifts at Christmas had already begun to be practiced in Italy when World War II (1939–1945) occurred. The American soldiers who were stationed there reinforced the custom. They brought Santa Claus (not to be confused with Italy's Saint Nicholas) and often decorated Christmas trees, as well.

Christmas trees today are very popular, especially in northern regions. Most are imported from northern Europe, but many families prefer an artificial tree—it lasts longer. Others buy live, potted trees that can be replanted after the holidays. Southern Italians sometimes decorate trees with fresh fruit and foil-covered chocolates. Children love these trees because on January 6 they are allowed to eat the trimmings.

In some regions, New Year's Day is another time for gifts, just as it was in ancient Rome. Long ago, a Yule log, called a *ceppo*, was dragged

During World War II, an American serviceman dressed as Santa Claus hands out Christmas gifts to children at a party at the Vatican.

in from the woods and set afire with much ceremony. Often the children were blindfolded, and they would hit the log with sticks or tongs, causing sparks to fly up. When the blindfolds were removed, a pile of gifts would magically have appeared for each child. The ashes of the burned log were kept as a charm against storms.

Later, the ceppo changed its shape, becoming a wood or cardboard pyramid with several shelves. It is gilded or covered with colored, fringed paper, and candles are attached to the sides. Gilded cherubs, pine cones, stars, birds, and other ornaments are added as decoration. One shelf holds the family's manger scene; others are for presents and perhaps a few family treasures.

New Year's Eve in most cities is celebrated with dazzling displays of fireworks. They are usually not planned civic events, but individual shows from rooftops, balconies, and street corners. Although fire-crackers are illegal, and highly dangerous, the authorities find it difficult to enforce the law that bans them.

The noise made by swooshing rockets and bursting firecrackers is, however, only the beginning. Many joyful celebrants shoot guns, sometimes with live ammunition. And—especially in Naples—the night is made even livelier by the sound of many objects crashing to the sidewalk from windows above.

Neapolitans hurl just about anything—preferably breakable items—from their windows: bottles, pots and pans, old clothes, bicycles, furniture, even a bathtub or two. All this sound and fury goes back to the days when evil spirits were believed to be abroad at this time of the year. Fire—and lots of noise—scared the demons away.

A gigantic white ox leads a parade through the streets of Bologna on New Year's Eve. It is the procession of the *bue grasso*, the fat ox. The animal is decorated from his giant horns to his tail with multicolored ribbons and flowers. The procession ends just before midnight at the square of San Petronio. From a nearby hill a cannon roars, the great clock in the square strikes 12, and thousands of onlookers light candles. Then fireworks light up the sky. In their midst a white flag appears. It is printed with the winning lottery number, and some lucky person has won the ox.

New Year's is the day on which Italian's believe they should try to do all of their favorite things, so that they may go on doing them all year. It is also the time for forecasting the future. Young girls burn olive leaves to find out whom they will marry, or they toss slippers over their shoulders at a door. If the slipper ends up pointing toward the outside, its owner will be married within the year.

The first person met on New Year's Day is very important, too. A strong, stalwart male, especially a sailor, is considered good luck. But if you meet a child, it might portend an early death. Meeting a priest first thing on New Year's Day is considered even worse luck, for that portends a funeral. And meeting a woman first is a disaster. Still today, there are Italian people who will not speak to a woman, even over the phone, first thing on January 1.

Epiphany is believed by many to be a time of wondrous happenings. Trees are suddenly covered with fruit, rivers and streams turn to gold, fountains flow with honey, and animals talk. In some regions, bonfires are kindled on the eve of Epiphany. The direction in which the smoke blows indicates the weather for the coming year.

Despite the growing trend toward giving gifts at Christmas, a large number of families still save their presents for Epiphany. Youngsters believe that a kindly old witch, La Befana, delivers the goodies. Even children who have received their real gifts on Christmas may get something on January 6—perhaps a stocking filled with candy.

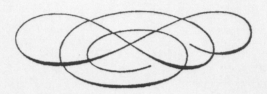

Festive markets

Abbondanza! That's Italian for "abundance," or "plenty." And Italy's fabulous Christmas markets certainly seem to have an abundance of everything! You can find practically any item you want, and a thousand things you don't.

Early in December, tables and wooden stalls in vast numbers appear in the central squares of towns large and small. They spread out into side streets, too, many of which are closed to automobile traffic for the season. Happy, jostling crowds wander about looking, sometimes buying, playing games of chance, and eating. The markets are really more like carnivals: noisy, gaudy, and fun.

Let's take a tour of some typical markets, beginning with Milan's sprawling Sant' Ambrogio Fair. Like the others, it offers a marvelous variety of wares for sale: manger figures, Christmas ornaments and toys, clothes, and gifts. Vendors cry the merits of all manner of used goods, too, from incomplete sets of dishes to chipped Caruso records and "antiques" of recent vintage. Doorknobs and copper pans, old books and maps, even beat-up sewing machines and typewriters, rugs, more-or-less usable furniture, pictures, and mirrors are optimistically offered to the browsing shoppers who stroll by.

A Christmas market in Bolzano, in the Trentino-Alto Adige region.

A spectacular night-time scene, this is the famous Christmas market in Rome's historic Piazza Navona. Crowds of people wander through the huge square, past long rows of booths overflowing with goods of all kinds.

Artists may be seen rapidly sketching caricatures or showing off their landscapes or religious paintings. Balloon sellers hawk their wares, a favorite balloon shape being the rabbit. Children toss balls and attempt to knock down rows of figures in game booths. The lucky winners can take home a stuffed animal—maybe a teddy bear. Bands of roving musicians, always a part of any Italian fair, fill the air with their lively music.

Booths and pushcarts do a brisk business in flowers. Poinsettias, cyclamens, azaleas, and violets bloom in colorful profusion everywhere. Bunches of holly and mistletoe wrapped in cellophane, all ready to hang on doors, are also big sellers.

Things to eat—on the spot or to take home—tempt shoppers at every turn. The chestnut vendor has a lot of customers; his stove is a good place to warm up chilled fingers. A popular Christmastime snack is a sandwich made with a slice of *porchetta*—a kind of roasted pork.

Countless stalls offer Christmas candy—chocolate, gum drops, licorice, and many other kinds of candy, as well. One favorite Christmas candy sold is a type of nougat called *torrone*. Other vendors sell dried fruit and nuts, and sticky cones of spun sugar.

Food shop owners on the streets near the market vie with the open-air booths for attention by creating marvelous window displays. Pastry shops present trays of delectable cakes and cookies, good-smelling breads, and brightly wrapped boxes of *panettone*, Italy's traditional Christmas cake. Rabbits, capons, turkeys, and hams hang in the butcher's window, bedecked with greenery.

Next door there is an enticing selection of big spiced sausages—salami, prosciutto, and capicolli. Then, an irresistible mountain of cheese catches the eye or maybe an arrangement of fruit: pears, strawberries, apricots, oranges, and apples. They appear so real one has to look twice to see that they are made of marzipan. Real fruit is also sold, of course, set out in beautiful, gleaming pyramids.

In Venice, Florence, and Rome, huge wholesale fish markets open their doors to the public for only a day or so just before Christmas. People stand, patiently waiting, until the official ceremonies are over. Then the markets become scenes of frantic activity as last-minute shoppers haggle with vendors over the prices of live eels and other fishy purchases.

Candy dolls in a charming assortment of guises are a tradition in Palermo's December market. Bologna's bustling Santa Lucia Market is set up under the portals of the Gothic Church of Santa Maria dei Servi. And Naples holds torchlight parades and fireworks displays in the Fondaco di San Gregorio Armeno, a small square near the waterfront.

One of the noisiest, most picturesque markets of all is held in Rome's Piazza Navona, beginning around December 15. The huge, historic square was once a center for holiday revelry with the ancient Romans. Chariot races took place there; it was even converted into a lake for small-scale naval battles. Today, three impressive fountains adorn the center of the piazza. Hundreds of kiosks, all jammed tightly together, are set up in long rows down the sides. Their roofs are painted in bright colors—orange and blue, red, yellow and green—rainbow stripes offering a cheerful contrast to the gloomy gray of the winter sky.

There is also a large outdoor Nativity scene, which attracts thousands of visitors. Shortly before Christmas, the auxiliary bishop of Rome appears on the balcony of the Braschi Palace overlooking the piazza.

He blesses the square, then comes down and walks its entire length, accompanied by a retinue of clergy and civil dignitaries.

When they reach the manger they offer prayers, and the display is declared officially open. The Nativity scene is built by the municipality of Rome, and each year a different artist is entrusted with its design. On the year of the moon landing it portrayed a moonscape, Earth, and the three astronauts. Another year, the scene consisted of a huge bubble with carved figures representing Joseph, Mary, and the Christ child.

On the last night of the fair, January 5—the eve of Epiphany—the Piazza Navona swarms with shoppers. It seems as though all of Rome descends upon this one square. Thousands of people mill about: tourists, Italian families en masse, couples out for an evening's entertainment, individuals of all sorts.

Merchants offer alluring bargains, hoping to sell out before tearing down their booths. Shoppers and sightseers good-naturedly push their way through the crowded aisles. Parents search for one last toy and, quite often, a lost child. Pretty girls pretend to ignore the flirtatious attentions of handsome youths.

Children race through the swirling mass, yelling and creating an earsplitting racket with toy whistles and trumpets. Grandmothers dicker fiercely with shouting vendors; old men and young wave their arms as they bellow greetings to friends. The musicians increase their decibel rate in happy competitions, and the din becomes deafening. It is a cheerful madhouse, exhausting and fun—and an absolutely essential element of the Roman holidays.

A stall from the market at Bolzano (see page 19), *where many beautiful Christmas decorations are displayed.*

A Christmas market in Garda, in the Venetia region.

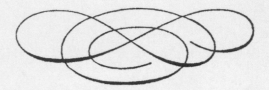

The legend of La Befana

It is the eve of Epiphany—the night of magic—when anything can happen. It is terribly hard for children to go to sleep on this night. But now they are tucked snugly in bed, dreaming of the exciting morning to come. Stockings, empty and waiting, hang by the fire. Everything is quiet; the house is very still.

Across the dark winter sky a strange figure flies like the wind. For a brief moment it is silhouetted against the moon. The figure pauses in its flight, then dives swiftly earthward. Whoosh! Down the chimney it pops. Quickly, it checks to make certain the children are sound asleep. Reassured, it cackles happily as it fills the stockings from a bulging sack.

It is a witch! She is very, very old and bent, dressed all in black. Her white hair is long and straggly, her nose is hooked, and she rides a broomstick. Her name is La Befana and she, not Santa Claus, traditionally brings gifts to the children of Italy.

A La Befana doll in colorful native costume watches passers-by from a market stall in the Piazza Navona (see page 20) *in Rome.*

La Befana pays her annual visit on January 6, the date when the Three Kings offered their gifts of gold, frankincense, and myrrh to the new-born Christ child in Bethlehem.

During the weeks preceding Epiphany, many youngsters write notes to La Befana telling her the presents that they would most like to receive. Girls and boys in Italy have to watch their manners as Epiphany draws near, because La Befana knows what the children have been up to. Tradition says ill-behaved youngsters just might awaken on the morning of Epiphany to find a lump of coal in their stockings instead of candy and toys. Most of the time, however, what looks like lumps of coal are really pieces of black-colored sugar candy.

In some parts of Italy, children gather on the eve of Epiphany to beat drums and blow whistles to welcome La Befana. Once home, before the children go to bed, they may leave out a small meal for La Befana.

La Befana's story begins at the time of Christ's birth. According to legend, the Three Kings journeyed through Italy on their way to Bethlehem. They stopped to ask directions of an old woman who was sweeping out her cottage, and they invited her to join them.

"I can't," she snapped gruffly. "I'm much too busy. And I've never heard of Bethlehem."

So the caravan moved on, the old woman staring thoughtfully after it. Shaking her head, she returned to her sweeping, trying to put the exotic travelers out of her mind. But she was lonely. Her husband had died long years before. She had always loved children and often wished she had some around to keep her company. Now there was a very special child, far away in some place called Bethlehem. Wherever that was.

"I'll go after all!" she cried. "If I hurry, perhaps I can catch up with them. I want to see the Christ child, too, and bring Him a gift!"

And so, she set out with her broom and a sack of goodies for the infant Jesus. The way was long and difficult, and the old woman

A child's representation of La Befana dropping gifts from the sky.

Children in a candy shop in Florence gaze at an array of treats they hope La Befana will leave for them.

soon was lost. She never did find the caravan, nor did she ever reach Bethlehem. Yet, so the story relates, she never gave up trying to find the Christ child. La Befana still searches even today, after all these centuries.

She flies around on her broom on the eve of Epiphany. Whenever she comes to a house where there is a child, she drops in to see if this child might be the one she seeks. It never is, but she leaves a gift anyway. For La Befana has come to realize, over the years, that her searching is not in vain, that in some way the Christ child can be found in each and every child she visits.

The origins of this Italian Christmas witch are uncertain. In about the 1100's and 1200's, Epiphany parades and songs featuring the Three Kings became popular in western Europe. In Italy and some other regions, gift giving became associated with the holiday in honor of the Three Kings who brought gifts to the Christ child. The stories about La Befana may also date to that time. In the mid-1500's, a poet from the northern Italian region of Tuscany, Agnolo Firenzuola, mentioned the witch in one of his poems. This mention seems to be the first time she was called "La Befana." The name "Befana" comes from "Epifania," the Italian name for Epiphany.

Some customs concerning La Befana may also originate in pre-Christian rituals. One such ritual was to burn a straw image of an old lady as a symbol of the ending of the old year and the beginning of a new one. The old woman symbolizes the barren land during winter. Her image is burned to make way for a fertile spring. It may be that this custom is continued in the popular Italian tradition of burning a puppet of La Befana in the town square on January 6.

La Befana

La Befana comes at night	*La Befana vien di notte*
In tattered shoes	*Con le scarpe tutte rotte*
Dressed in the Roman style	*Col vestito alla romana*
Long live La Befana!	*Viva viva La Befana !*
She brings cinders and coals	*Porta cenere e carboni*
To the naughty children	*Ai bambini cattivoni*
To the good children	*Ai bambini belli e buoni*
She brings sweets and lots of gifts!	*Porta chicchi e tanti doni!*

A woman dressed as La Befana making polenta at a Christmas market.

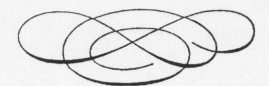

Art of the Nativity

The story of Christ's birth has inspired countless artists through the centuries. In Italy, where religion has always played such an important role, representations of the Nativity have been created in many forms: in paintings and sculpture, mosaics and enamel, and in stained-glass windows.

Manuscript illuminators also used the Nativity theme in ornamental initials at the start of a chapter, in border designs, or for full-page illustrations. (Illuminated manuscripts are books that were written out and illustrated by hand. This art form flourished from the 500's until into the 1400's.) The glowing, colorful scenes in these books often gleamed with added touches of gold and silver. An example of illumination may be seen on the facing page. It shows Mary, Joseph, and the Infant Jesus in the stable, watched over by animals and angels in the background.

A page from an illuminated manuscript depicting the Nativity.

A relief showing a Nativity scene, created in Milan around 1400.

Nativity portrayals during the first few hundred years of the Christian era were rare. A few were carved on the walls of the catacombs beneath Rome, where the early Christians hid from their persecutors. One such relief (sculpture in which the figures or designs project from their background) shows the Christ child in His crib, with shepherds and the Three Kings nearby.

In later years, Italy's greatest painters and sculptors often chose Biblical themes—including the story of the Nativity—for their work. In the 1200's, the Pisano family of sculptors included the Nativity in carved panels for churches. In the 1300's, the Florentine painter and sculptor Giotto portrayed the Madonna and Child, Joseph, shepherds, and angels in some frescoes (paintings made on damp plaster, using pigments mixed with water).

In a fresco by Fra Angelico—a famed Dominican monk and painter from the 1400's—the Holy Family is shown.

During the early Renaissance (in the 1400's), the della Robbia family depicted the manger scene in some of their richly colored terra cotta (ceramic clay) medallions, used as architectural ornaments. In the 1400's and 1500's, Fra Angelico, Botticelli, Michelangelo, Tintoretto, and many others painted the Madonna and Child and other Biblical scenes, such as the flight into Egypt or the shepherds and Wise Men worshiping at Christ's manger.

Neapolitan sculptors in the 1600's and 1700's retold the ancient Christmas story with their marvelous miniature figures and settings for the manger scenes, called *presepi* (from the Italian word *presepio*, meaning stable or manger). Even today there are superb woodcarvers and makers of beautiful papier mâché figures who carry on the great tradition.

Italy's glassmakers have been masters of their art for many centuries, creating clear or colored goblets, vases, bowls, and beads. Venetian glass, manufactured in family-owned shops on the island of Murano, is famous the world over. Glass blowing in Venice began more than 1,000 years ago.

When the Christmas tree became popular in Italy, the glass blowers turned their talents toward making ornaments and created a new form of Christmas art. The fragile glass balls, stars—and other shapes—sometimes have a lacy pattern running through them. Other ornaments may be transparent with a tiny object inside. Still others are adorned with designs or textured surfaces. Or, ornaments may be fashioned to look like hard candies that have been wrapped in beautifully colored cellophane. The ornaments made on Murano are all exquisite—some of the loveliest ornaments to be found anywhere.

Not only great masters and skilled craftsmen, however, portray the joy of Christmas. There are the delightful homemade manger scenes lovingly fashioned of simple materials with a great deal of ingenuity and artistry. And there are the drawings made by Italian children at home or in school. All the many aspects of the Christmas season in Italy come to vivid life in these paintings: manger scenes, Christmas trees, presents, holiday meals with the family, and winter landscapes. Christmas art made by children may be the most charming of all.

A Nativity scene created by Giovanni della Robbia of the celebrated family of sculptors. The figures were composed of terra cotta and then glazed in glowing colors.

Beautiful glass ornaments made in Venice, on the island of Murano.

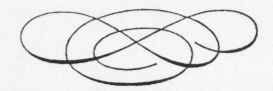

Christmas mangers

It was the winter of 1223. Christmas was coming, and a man named Francis was busily preparing a novel celebration near Assisi, high in the snow-covered Umbrian hills.

Francis (later Saint Francis) was born in 1181 or 1182, the son of a wealthy Assisi merchant. As a youth, he had thoroughly enjoyed the good things money and position could bring. At age 20, he became a soldier and was captured. During his imprisonment, he fell ill and believed that he heard voices. They told him he must change his way of life, give up his possessions, and go out into the world to preach the word of Christ.

Francis obeyed. He devoted himself to helping lepers and other outcasts, and he worked at restoring ruined churches. Barefoot and in rags, he traveled to far-distant lands, including Palestine, where he visited the birthplace of Christ.

A Neapolitan artist surrounded by his manger figurines. His shop is in San Gregorio Armeno Street, where most of the crib artists of Naples practice their craft.

Francis was a remarkable man, holy, humble, and yet full of joy and bursting with eagerness to share his beliefs. He once wrote that he wished he could speak to the emperor. He would, he said, request that Christmas be shared by all, even the birds and other animals. Crumbs should be scattered on all the roadways on the anniversary of Jesus's birth, and oxen and donkeys should be given an extra ration of food.

But, Francis's greatest desire was that people, all people, might share his wonder at the miracle of the birth of Christ. He wanted his followers to witness the story as it really had happened, to show them that Christ came from simple beginnings, just as they did.

So, Francis sent a message to Giovanni Vellita, a nobleman of the region. Vellita, who greatly respected Francis, came as fast as he could. He was a rather fat man, and he arrived huffing and puffing, red-faced from the exertion.

"What can I do for you, my friend?" Vellita wheezed.

"I want you to help arrange a celebration," Francis told him. "I would like to show how the infant Jesus was born in Bethlehem, how He suffered from cold and lack of proper shelter, and how He lay in the manger warmed only by the breath of the ox and ass."

Vellita was delighted with the plan. He provided a manger filled with hay—and live animals, too. All the people of the countryside were invited, and they came carrying torches and candles. The friars sang hymns as Francis celebrated the Mass under the stars that Christmas Eve. In his own words, he related the old, old story of Jesus's birth.

As he spoke, the shepherds came, and Mary and Joseph—all acted by people from the village. There were sheep, too, and an ass and ox. The watchers must have felt that they had been transported back in time— more than 1,200 years—to that original manger scene. Francis gently placed a small wax figure of Jesus in the manger. He was so moved by the beauty of it all that he wept with joy.

Francis died in 1226. Two years later, he was declared a saint and eventually was named patron saint of all Italy. His small group of monks became the Franciscan order of the Roman Catholic Church. And his modest little reenactment of the Gospel story grew into a Christmas tradition beloved in Italy and in many other countries around the world. It is called a *crèche* in French and a *nacimiento* in Spanish.

The participants in the first live presepio enjoyed it so much that they repeated it year after year. Soon other towns took it up—and the custom spread. And someone, somewhere, had the idea of creating a presepio using small, carved figures. One of the earliest known manger scenes of this type appeared around the end of the 1200's, in Rome's Church of Santa Maria Maggiore. It still exists today.

At first, the scenes were simple and included only Jesus, Joseph, and Mary. The figures were usually crude, made of wood or clay. In the mid-1600's, the nobility became captivated by the presepi. The best artists available were commissioned to produce mangers, and they were no longer merely Nativity groupings. Other Biblical tales were added, and the background began to portray typical Italian scenes, complete with bustling, crowded streets, or sheep-dotted mountainsides.

The Spanish Prince Charles of Bourbon became king of Naples in 1734, as Charles IV. He was fascinated by the miniature reproductions

and enjoyed designing elaborate settings for them. Some say he even carved a few of the figures himself. His queen, Maria Amalia, sewed exquisite costumes for the figures using lace and rich fabrics, and real jewels.

By the late 1700's, the Neapolitan presepi reached heights of splendor and intricacy that have never since been equaled. Noble lords and ladies visited each other's houses to compare the lavish productions. A manger sometimes would occupy an entire room or even sprawl into adjacent rooms.

The tiny figures were completely realistic. Each small human was dressed according to occupation or rank and in the fashion of the times, from great ladies and gentlemen down to the humblest villager. Men sat in a tavern twirling spaghetti on forks and housewives haggled with vendors. Animals wandered amiably through the streets, a donkey lay down and rolled in the grass, a cow scratched with her hind leg.

Real waterfalls tumbled down hillsides, and fountains gushed real water. In some presepi, Mount Vesuvius could be seen erupting in the background. The scenes were fantastic and exuberant—vivid reproductions of Neapolitan life and masterpieces of the sculptor's art.

Fortunately, many of those magnificent, centuries-old presepi may still be seen. Some are on permanent display in museums or are reassembled at Christmastime in the great churches of Italy. King Charles's splendid exhibit, with 1,200 individual pieces, is in the Royal Palace of Caserta.

In Rome, one of the most impressive Christmas cribs may be visited at the Basilica of Saints Cosmos and Damian, near the Coliseum. It was created more than 200 years ago in Naples. The crib is 45 feet long, 21 feet wide, and 27 feet high, it contains hundreds of hand-carved wooden figures.

Rome has the most famous Christ child, too, the revered Santo Bambino, in the Church of Santa Maria in Ara Coeli. The little figure is encrusted with precious jewels; its lifelike coloring is supposed to have

The Holy Family depicted in a Neapolitan presepio.

A section of a presepio (previous page) donated to the Museo di San Martino, in Naples, in the late 1800's. This elaborate Neapolitan presepio includes hundreds of figures. Here, a tavern-keeper serves food to his guests.

been added by angels' hands. According to legend, a monk carved it of wood from the Mount of Olives in the Holy Land. The figure is believed to have miraculous healing powers. Once it was stolen, the story goes, but managed to return all by itself, waking up the friars by ringing the church bells and knocking loudly on the door. Supposedly, the small figure scolded them for having been so careless.

Believers write letters to the figure, asking for special favors. The mail is always delivered, even if the address is only "Bambino, Roma." Every Christmas Eve, the little figure is taken from its niche and placed into a manger within the church. A platform is erected before it, where Roman children stand to deliver short sermons or sing. They are seldom shy about performing, speaking out with dramatic aplomb, often adding an encore at the slightest sign of encouragement.

In some regions, there are animated presepio, usually with large, almost life-sized, figures. In Milan, one is erected in a structure next to the Duomo. It is hard to know where to begin looking: on one side a woodsman cuts a tree, by the river two fishermen haul out their catch. Washerwomen farther upstream pound and scrub their laundry, while children in a village chase chickens and dogs. On a small lake, a sailboat bounces on the choppy waves, and skiers swoop down snow-clad mountains in the background. Even the lighting changes, from sunny to cloudy to dusky, and then the moon and stars appear.

"Living" mangers are popular, too, with live participants portraying the various characters in the Nativity tale. They are like Saint Francis's

reenactment, but with more people. Many villages, including Rivisondoli, in the mountains of Abruzzi, put on a living presepio each year.
Everyone in Rivisondoli participates in the show, and there may be as
many as 600 actors. Others join in, too: vacationers who have come for
the skiing often sign up for coveted roles, especially that of the Virgin.

Preparations begin weeks in advance with rounding up as many
people as possible who own one of the beautiful regional costumes.
Animals, too, are needed. The actors do not get paid for performing,
but the animals or, rather, their owners—do. The show begins in the
late afternoon of January 5, and huge crowds gather to watch.

Rivisondoli lies at an altitude of almost 4,000 feet. At this time of
year, the ground is usually deep in snow, and often more snow is falling.
It is dark, but spotlights from below trace the actors' path as they move
slowly down the mountainside. There are shepherds galore, mostly real
ones, as this is a region of shepherds. Some of the villagers bring gifts—
fruit, live chickens, pigs or lambs—for the Infant Jesus. The Three
Kings ride down on horses. To play a king is a very great honor, so the
roles are customarily allotted to the mayors of nearby villages.

Finally, Mary appears astride a donkey. She carries a real baby, and
Joseph walks proudly at her side. Sheep mill about in large numbers; an
ox and ass stand patiently waiting. It is a colorful, moving spectacle,
ending at a humble manger set inside a shallow cave.

After its peak in the 1600's and 1700's, the practice of creating
enormous, costly presepi almost died out. But in this century, interest

43

in the manger scenes sprang up again. And at Christmastime today, it seems as though all of Italy is one giant presepio. Many people work to preserve the mangers created in the past and to promote the art of making new ones.

Contests for the best crib displays are held throughout the country, in schools, places of business, and town halls. Nativity scenes are erected virtually everywhere—not only in homes and churches, villages and city squares, but in gas stations and post offices, airports, and railway depots. Shop windows offer unique versions, some made entirely of pastry and some carved out of butter. There are presepi made of shells or seeds, bread dough, and even fruit.

Children make mangers as school projects, from cardboard, papier mâché or, in one case, from old bottles and used light bulbs. Smaller mangers are often installed inside old television sets. Like big shadow boxes, they offer depth for better perspective—and they are portable! Manger figures range from life-size to some so tiny that they fit into a nutshell.

After the procession, the Santo Bambino is placed in a manger (left), where the figure will be displayed until Epiphany.

The presepio is set up sometime during the weeks before Christmas. Most families purchase a few new figures at the market each year. Some markets sell nothing else. Presepi are like sets of electric trains— one never has enough pieces. Many families hand valuable figures down from generation to generation. Other presepi may be made of cardboard or plastic, but all are cherished.

Until Christmas Eve, the manger lies empty. Then, with great ceremony, the Bambino is laid in His crib. Some households have two sets of the Three Kings; one reenacts their caravan journey, the second kneels before the manger. Other families move the little figures as the days pass, allowing the Kings to reach the stable exactly on January 6. On Epiphany or shortly after, the presepio is dismantled and carefully put away till next year.

The presepi of Italy may have changed through the years since Saint Francis's simple version. His affection for the original Nativity scene in Bethlehem, however, is still very much alive in the hearts of Italians today.

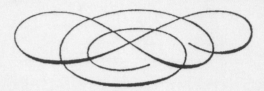

Music from the hills

It is believed that the first church bells ever used in a Christian service were Italian, and that they pealed out on a Christmas Eve about 1,600 years ago. Until then, the faithful had been called to Mass by a man going around the community ringing a handbell.

Bishop Paulinus of Nola (354?–431), in the province of Campania, is credited with instituting the custom of using church bells, instead. Since then, the joyous clangor of bells has become associated with Christmas everywhere. And in Italy today, at midnight on Christmas Eve, all the country's churches ring out the glad tidings, "Christ is born!"

The most characteristic Italian Christmas sound, however, is not that of bells, but of bagpipes. Sometime around the middle of December, the noisy market in Rome's Piazza Navona shrills with a new sound: the bagpipers have arrived!

Called *zampognari*, they are musicians—at one time, nearly all were shepherds—who live high in the mountains and come down each year at Christmastime to perform in the market and at other sites in Rome. They visit other cities and towns, too, particularly in the regions of Calabria, Abruzzi, and Molise. The melodies they play are adaptations of old hill tunes, such as the shepherd song, "Cantata dei Pastori."

A solitary bagpiper plays a Christmas melody in a misty Sicilian street.

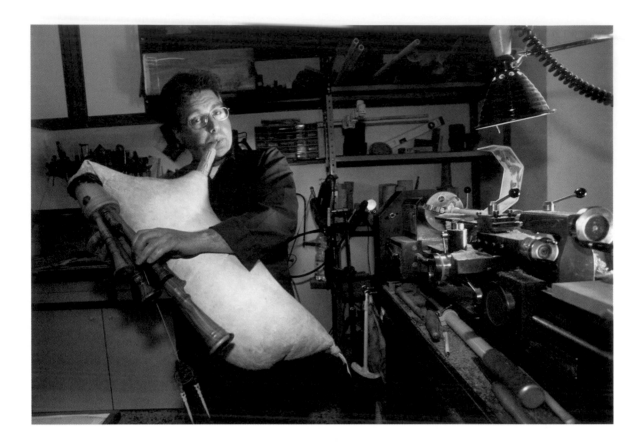

A bagpipe maker plays the pipes in his workshop in the Calabria region.

Most people think of bagpipes as Scottish or Irish, but they have long been found in one form or another in many lands. In Italy, bagpipes date to the time of the ancient Romans. Legend says that shepherds, who traditionally play the bagpipes, entertained Mary in Bethlehem long ago. She supposedly preferred their strange, droning music to any other. One story claims that thoughtful shepherds even eased her labor pains with their melodies. Because of these legends, shepherds with bagpipes are often featured in Italian manger scenes.

In years past, the zampognari made a practice of stopping before every shrine to the Madonna and every Nativity scene. There they would serenade the Virgin Mother. They also paid visits to carpenters' shops to honor Joseph's memory.

In some regions, the zampognari and *pifferari,* "flutists," would go from door to door and knock. They would ask if the householder wished them to return for the novena, the nine days of special prayers before Christmas. If the answer was yes, they would leave a wooden spoon or mark the doorway in some manner.

Later, when the musicians came back for the Christmas novena, they would gather to sing and to play in front of the family's manger scene. Money or food was paid to the musicians in exchange for their

A lone shepherd with his flock in the Abruzzi region.

Pastori

In general, shepherds take care of a flock of sheep. They help a sheep if it becomes ill or injured. Shepherds may assist a ewe (female sheep) that is having difficulty *lambing* (giving birth). They also protect their sheep from predators. Shepherds sometimes shear their sheep of their fleece.

In some regions of Italy, shepherds—called *pastori*—were especially important at one time. In mountainous areas, a type of agriculture known as *transhumance* is often practiced. That means that livestock are moved from upland to lowland pastures, depending upon the season. In the summer months, areas in lower parts of such Italian regions as Apulia are very dry and hot. There is very little grass for sheep to graze on. During those months, the practice evolved of taking the sheep high up into the mountains

into such regions of the Apennines as Abruzzi and Molise, where it was cooler and grass was more plentiful. In winter, however, such areas are cold and snow-covered. So, in fall, shepherds led their flocks back down the mountain to winter in the lowlands. The shepherds were needed to help these large groups of sheep to safely move up and down the mountainside. This seasonal migration of livestock goes back to ancient times in Italy, probably at least 2,000 years.

By the late 1800's, however, this system began to be less and less common in the Italian countryside. People began leaving the countryside and moving to the cities. Italy became a more industrial and less agricultural nation. Today, there are still some shepherds, but they are far fewer in number than they were in the past. Zampognari in Rome today are more likely to be folk musicians keeping Christmas traditions alive than the traditional shepherds of Italy.

Musicians in the Piazza Navona in Rome (above); *two generations of zampognari pipe their shepherd tunes* (right).

In Milan, two children accompany their parents.

services. In Sicily, the shepherds would sometimes be accompanied by a violinist or a cellist.

Modern-day zampognari still dress much as their ancestors did, and they are a fascinating sight in their shaggy sheepskin vests, leather breeches, or sheepskin leggings. Over their shoulders, they wear long woolen cloaks, and their white stockings are bound by leather thongs reaching up to the knees. Today, zampognari are not as likely to be actual shepherds as they once were. Changes in farming practices have diminished the number of shepherds in Italy. Today's zampognari may be folk musicians who learned how to play the pipes in order to keep alive the customs and traditions of the culture of their region of Italy.

At one time, the zampognari walked all the way down from their mountain meadows to perform. Nowadays, most of the musicians drive cars, ride motor scooters, or take a bus or train from their mountain home. Still, their arrival is a cheerful announcement that the Christmas season has arrived.

51

Tastes of the season

There is no such thing as a "typical" Christmas menu in Italy. Traditional foods and methods of cooking vary widely throughout the country's 20 regions. The different styles have one thing in common, though. They are all excellent.

Italian housewives make a point of choosing only the freshest ingredients for their kitchens. Several trips to the market are necessary, and the process of selection is taken seriously. It is accomplished, usually with much discussion between wary purchaser and eager seller. Husbands often accompany their wives, offering critical advice as to which eel is the fattest, dismissing this pear or that artichoke as having too many spots. And that is only the beginning!

Next come long hours of preparation: making pasta by hand, simmering sauces, creating a number of desserts, and more. Each dish is made with a generous hand—no skimping in Italian cooking. Some of the results will be shared with friends and neighbors; the rest will disappear, like magic, during the holidays.

Many Italians observe a rigid 24-hour fast that ends on Christmas Eve, so appetites are whetted to their sharpest on that night. The table is set with the family's finest linens, china, and silver. Even in the poorer homes, this is the one time of the year when no one will stint, when an elaborate banquet of all the traditional foods must be served.

The Christmas Eve meal begins around seven or eight o'clock and usually lasts for several hours. By ancient custom, it is meatless. In Naples and other parts of southern Italy, a large female eel, *capitone*, is served, with various sauces, as the main course. Eel is also popular in areas as far north as Chioggia, near Venice, where the best eels are bred. They are sold live at the market, and depending on the area or the family tradition, are roasted, baked, fried, or steamed with rice. Along the seacoast, *calamari*, or squid, is the favored delicacy. *Vongoli*, small clams, are another common Christmas Eve offering, as is *baccalà*, codfish.

Selecting just the right fish at a market in Venice.

There will also be vegetables: some dipped in fritter batter and deep-fried *(fritto misto)*, beans of many kinds, and perhaps an assortment of vegetables pickled in vinegar. Salads, too, are served, and usually a colorful platter of *antipasto* (an assortment of various

appetizers). Crusty loaves of bread and pasta in countless shapes and sizes round out the meal, which is followed by sweets and caffé espresso. Wine always accompanies the supper, often ending with Asti Spumanti—a sparkling (bubbly) wine. Afterward, nearly everyone goes to Midnight Mass, well fed and ready to thoroughly enjoy the beautiful holy night services.

Others attend church the next morning, and Christmas dinner is served shortly after noon. In many families the children, using their best penmanship, write special letters for this occasion. The letters are then hidden somewhere on the table, under Papa's plate or perhaps tucked inside a napkin. In them, the youngsters ask forgiveness for any misdeeds they may have committed and promise to be very, very good in the coming year.

Papa pretends to see nothing unusual about the table, despite all the excited giggling going on. Suddenly he spies a not-too-well-concealed note.

"What's this?" he asks with a great show of astonishment. "A letter for Mama and me?"

He then proceeds to read the letter aloud, with much dramatic fervor. Mama beams, battling a tear or two of maternal pride. Grand-

parents utter cries of admiration, and even older brothers and sisters applaud the young ones' efforts.

Christmas dinner, like most Italian meals, starts off with soup—usually *tortellini in brodo* (broth). Tortellini, generally homemade, are little pasta casings that are stuffed with such fillings as a spiced-meat mixture. In Sicily, roast turkey is preferred as a main course; in other regions, a baked, stuffed ham is served. Lentils with sausage will often appear as a side dish. Lentils may also be served on New Year's Day. Once they symbolized money, and in some areas even today it is believed that eating them will guarantee a year of prosperity and good luck.

A holiday dessert staple in almost every region of Italy nowadays is *panettone*, once found only in Milan. Made with currants and candied fruit, it is a yeast cake, very light and high, baked in a fluted pan and then glazed. Making panettone from scratch is a lengthy process, so people often buy a commercial brand. Panettone is sold in almost every kind of shop and is a popular gift item at Christmastime.

Amaretti, almond macaroons, are favorite sweets, as are *cannoli*, crisp pastry shells filled with creamy ricotta cheese, whipped cream, and candied fruit. There are *strufoli,* too, little balls

Apples, pears, peaches, and other fruits (shown above)—realistic though they appear, all the fruits are actually candy, cleverly formed from marzipan and tinted by hand. And, an Italian favorite, a type of crisp cookie called biscotti (below).

of dough fried in oil and as light as a feather. They are dipped in honey, sprinkled with colored sugar beads, and eaten with the fingers.

Delicate sweets called *pinocchiati*, made with pine nuts, are a central Italian specialty, particularly in the region of Umbria. The province of Siena invented spicy *panforte* back in the Middle Ages. Today it is available all over the country. It is more candy than cake, solid with fruit and nuts, and very chewy.

Sicilian cooks are renowned for their delectable desserts, and their masterpiece is the luscious *cassata*, a sponge cake with a filling of ricotta, candied fruit, almonds, grated chocolate, and rum.

Fruit, nuts, and candy are always offered at the end of the meal. Sweets and fruits, now served so lavishly, were once very special treats in Italy. Often Christmas was the only time of the year when one could afford to eat them.

A great many Italian candies and desserts are made with nuts and honey. People once believed that nuts could ensure fertile fields, flocks, and families. And in the time of the ancient Romans, honey was thought to have almost magical properties. It was often given as a present, especially at New Year's, so that "the coming year would be as sweet as the gift."

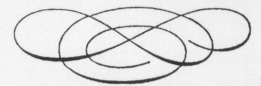

Christmas at the Vatican

Within the city of Rome lies another country: Vatican City. It extends over only about 109 acres (44 hectares), and its gardens, courtyards, and magnificent buildings are almost completely surrounded by walls. The museums and chapels of the Vatican Palace contain some of the world's greatest works of art. St. Peter's Basilica is a huge church that looks out over a vast square. Headquarters of the Roman Catholic Church, the Vatican is also the official residence of the pope.

Since 1968, the pope has presided over a special ceremony for children on the last Sunday before Christmas. Thousands of youngsters bring their manger figure of Baby Jesus to St. Peter's Square to be blessed by the pope. While gathered in the square, the children sing Christmas songs. When John Paul II (1920–2005) observed his first Christmas as pope in 1978, more than 50,000 of Rome's schoolchildren came to the square. They serenaded John Paul with carols, including a Christmas song from his native Poland. The pope was delighted. Energetically conducting from his balcony, he sang right along with the youngsters.

Pope John Paul II opens the Holy Door in St. Peter's Basilica on December 24, 1999. The Holy Door is opened once every 25 years at Christmastime.

Christmas Eve Mass

In 1954, Pope Pius XII began the practice of broadcasting the Christmas Mass from the Vatican basilica. Over the years, the reach of the broadcast has grown steadily. At first, only European countries received the broadcast. In the early 1970's, the first satellite broadcasts from the Vatican made it possible for people in many more parts of the world to watch the Mass live.

Today, Midnight Mass from St. Peter's Basilica and the pope's traditional message on Christmas Day are televised live by more than 100 networks to more than 70 countries on 6 continents.

In addition to being shown on television, the telecast is now available live on the Internet, through the Vatican Web site. Also, beginning in 2004, cell phone users in several countries were able to see the Vatican Christmas concert and Midnight Mass on their cell phones.

John Paul II welcomes children in colorful costumes to the midnight Christmas Mass at the Basilica in 2004.

There has long been a special bond between popes and Italy's beloved manger scenes. Pope Honorius III (?–1227) gave Saint Francis permission to create his live Nativity scene, the first ever, way back in 1223. Paul VI (1897–1978), who became pope in 1963, was particularly fond of mangers. He ordered a new one for the Mathilde Chapel in the Vatican and placed the figure of the Christ child in the crib himself.

Pope Benedict XVI

In 1965, a children's Christmas party was given at the Vatican. The young guests were all winners of local manger contests. A large presepio with a lovely blue sky and lots of flying angels had been set up in the background. Paul VI entered the room where the party was held and spoke to the children about the meaning of the Nativity scene. Then the pope invited them to sit down for the holiday meal, and, to the youngsters' astonishment, he poured the soup into each child's bowl. After a festive lunch, the children offered the pope a live lamb. They played some games, too, and sang carols. Finally, three tall men entered the room, dressed in the gorgeous costumes of the Three Kings. Behind them walked a solemn camel—a real one, borrowed from the Roman zoo! On the camel's back was a large bag full of gifts from the pope. The children—and Paul VI, obviously—had a fine time.

Christmas in the Vatican is always a splendid occasion, rich with pageantry, music, incense, glowing colors, and precious jewels. The highlight is Midnight Mass on Christmas Eve, celebrated by the pope in St. Peter's. It is an incredibly impressive church, glittering with gold and filled with priceless paintings, statues, and mosaics. The main altar stands in the center, its bronze canopy *(baldacchino)* upheld by massive, ornate columns. And more than 400 feet (122 meters) overhead looms the awesome dome, designed by Michelangelo.

Around 10 p.m., the huge basilica slowly begins to fill with people. Photographers rush about busily preparing their cameras, setting up tripods, flashes, and floodlights. Television crews, too, bustle purposefully around their cameras mounted on movable scaffolds, trying out

Pope John Paul II gives the Benediction at the great central altar during Christmas Midnight Mass in St. Peter's.

A Christmas Door

Pope John Paul II enters the Holy Door at St. Peter's in 1999 (see also photo on page 59).

The northernmost of the five doors that form the main entrance to St. Peter's Basilica in Vatican City is a special door. Called the *Porta Santa* (meaning "Holy Door"), it is opened every 25 years at Christmastime.

The custom arose in connection with Jubilee years. A Jubilee year, also known as an *anno santo* (Holy Year), is a special time declared by the pope to encourage the deepening of Christian commitment among believers. During the Jubilee year, many Roman Catholic pilgrims travel to Rome. After confessing their sins and receiving Communion, they traditionally perform certain acts of devotion—visiting St. Peter's Basilica and the three other main churches of Rome—in order to obtain remission of (freedom from) the earthly punishment due for their sins. Today, believers may also visit other pilgrim sites and perform other acts of devotion in Jubilee years. But the time of Jubilee in Rome is still special.

Pope Boniface VIII proclaimed the first Roman Catholic Jubilee in 1300. Eventually, the Roman Catholic Church came to celebrate Jubilee years every 25 years, as well as in special years designated by the pope.

The tradition of opening the Holy Door to begin the Holy Year started with the Jubilee of 1500. Most of the time, the door is enclosed behind a wall of bricks and mortar. In the ritual opening of the door, the pope traditionally struck the masonry, loosened earlier by Vatican workers, with a silver hammer. But workers prepared for the start of the Jubilee of 2000 by removing the masonry. On Christmas Eve of 1999, Pope John Paul II sang, "Open to me, Gate of Justice; This is the Gateway of the Lord," and pushed open the door.

After a year, the pope ritually closes the Holy Door, which is sealed again with brick and mortar. An urn containing coins and a parchment giving the dates of the door's opening and closing is sealed into the wall. In another 25 years, a pope will unseal and open the door again on Christmas Eve.

A snowy day in St. Peter's Square.

different angles and positions. The services on this night will be televised via satellite all around the world.

As the hour advances, the pace quickens. The crowds become larger and the people seem to move faster. There are nuns, priests, and seminarians in great numbers. There are tourists and pilgrims from many lands—Africa, Australia, India, the Philippines. And there are Italians—young and old, rich and poor. The children, and there are many, are quite well behaved. Some move from one family member to another, trying to persuade someone to lift them up for a better view. Older boys and girls climb on columns or balustrades to see.

At 11 o'clock, the church is suddenly flooded with light and the music and the singing begin. Then, a sudden hush, followed by excited murmurs: "Here he comes!" Somebody has spotted the pope. But first come the cardinals, the Swiss guards in their colorful medieval costumes, the bishops, and a large retinue of priests. Then the pontiff appears, greeting and blessing the crowds on both sides of the aisle.

The pope arrives at the altar and begins to celebrate the Mass. It is a long service, with much singing of chants followed by responses. The pope delivers the sermon. He also personally gives Communion to several hundred worshipers. The rest of the multitude is served by his many assistants. Now the Mass is over, and the pope again crosses the entire length of the basilica. Everyone applauds vigorously, shouting, "Viva il Papa!"

The Holy Father proceeds slowly, acknowledging the warm, emotional reception with smiles and blessings. Some high-ranking dignitaries follow him into the sacristy. The rest of the crowd gradually files out of the church, into the chilly Christmas morning.

64

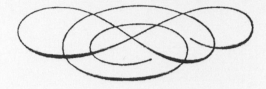

Buon Natale

The holiday season in Italy is a happy time, rich with religious feeling and spiced with lavish quantities of good things to eat. On the following pages you will find recipes for typical dishes and sweets from many regions, so that you can create your own authentic Italian Christmas feast.

Decorating the house is an important part of holiday fun in Italy, too. Quilling is one of the country's many delightful folk arts, and we have included easy-to-follow directions for making a charming quilled ornament for your Christmas tree. You will also find another enjoyable project for the whole family: a paper version of a stained-glass window.

Italy is a land of song, and no Italian Christmas would be complete without music. We have chosen two traditional carols—a Sicilian bagpipers' melody and the ever popular "From Starry Skies Thou Comest," written and composed by Saint Alphonsus Liguori (1696–1787).

A festively decorated house filled with family, friends, and song, and a holiday table laden with delicious food—that's an Italian Christmas. We wish you and yours Buon Natale!

Holiday treats

Lentils with sausage

1 cup lentils, rinsed
2 cups water
1 cup dry white wine
2 tablespoons olive oil
1 large tomato, peeled, seeded, and chopped
1 slice bacon, diced
1 clove garlic, chopped
6 peppercorns (withhold half for sausage mixture)
2 small bay leaves (withhold half for sausage mixture)
Salt to taste
2 pounds mild Italian sausage
1 small onion
1 small carrot, diced
1 stalk celery, cut in pieces

1. Combine lentils, water, wine, oil, tomato, bacon, garlic, 3 peppercorns, 1 bay leaf, and salt in a saucepan. Bring to boil, reduce heat, and simmer covered about 1 hour, or until lentils are soft.

2. Meanwhile, put sausage, onion, carrot, celery, and remaining peppercorns and bay leaf into a large saucepan. Add enough water to cover by 1 inch. Bring to boil, reduce heat, and simmer covered 30 minutes. Remove sausage from liquid, remove casing, and cut into thick slices.

3. Serve sausage slices with lentils.

   4 servings

Baked cod

2 pounds salted cod, cut in serving pieces
1 can (16 ounces) tomatoes, drained and sieved
1/4 cup chopped green olives
2 tablespoons capers
1 tablespoon snipped parsley
1/2 teaspoon salt
1/4 teaspoon pepper
1/2 teaspoon oregano

1. Soak salted cod in cold water in refrigerator for 24 hours, changing water every few hours.

2. Rinse with cold water and pat dry. Arrange pieces in a greased 2-quart baking dish.

3. Combine sieved tomatoes, olives, capers, parsley, and seasonings in a saucepan. Bring to boil. Pour sauce over fish.

4. Bake at 350 °F. for 25 to 30 minutes, or until fish flakes easily when tested with a fork.

4 to 6 servings

Sautéed scallops

1/4 cup butter or margarine
1 clove garlic
1 pound scallops
Salt
Freshly ground white peppercorns
Lemon wedges
Tartar sauce

1. Crush garlic with the flat side of a knife blade.

2. In skillet, melt butter or margarine. Add garlic. Heat until just brown, then remove garlic and discard.

3. Add scallops. Cook for 5 minutes. Season with salt and pepper.

4. Serve with lemon wedges and tartar sauce.

4 servings

Spaghetti with tuna

1/3 cup olive oil
1/3 cup butter
1 can (6 1/2 or 7 ounces) tuna, drained and flaked
1/4 cup snipped parsley
3 tablespoons water
1 pound spaghetti, cooked following package directions

1. Put oil, butter, tuna, and parsley into a small saucepan. Set over low heat for 3 or 4 minutes. Stir well. Add water and simmer 10 minutes.

2. Combine hot spaghetti and sauce and serve immediately.

   6 servings

Mixed fry of vegetables (fritto misto)

1 small eggplant, pared	3 tablespoons olive oil
4 small zucchini	3/4 cup warm water
Salt	4 ounces mozzarella
1 cup flour	1 egg white
1/4 teaspoon salt	Oil for frying

1. Cut eggplant in half crosswise, then cut lengthwise into 3-inch sticks. Cut zucchini into lengthwise sticks. Sprinkle salt over vegetables and allow to stand about 2 hours. Drain off liquid.

2. Put flour and 1/4 teaspoon salt into a bowl, add oil and water, and stir until smooth. Set aside 2 hours.

3. Slice cheese about 1/8-inch thick and cut into 3-inch lengths.

4. Heat a 1/2-inch depth of oil in a large skillet. If desired, use 2 skillets.

5. Just before using batter, beat egg white until soft peaks are formed and fold into batter until blended.

6. Dip some of the vegetable and cheese pieces into batter, then fry, a layer at a time, in hot oil until browned, turning as necessary. Drain on paper towels.

   6 servings

Cannoli

Filling:
2 pounds ricotta
2 teaspoons vanilla extract
1/2 cup confectioners' sugar
1/2 cup finely chopped
    candied citron
1/2 cup semisweet chocolate chips

Shells:
3 cups flour
1/4 cup sugar

1 teaspoon cinnamon
1/4 teaspoon salt
3 tablespoons shortening
2 eggs, well beaten
2 tablespoons white vinegar
2 tablespoons cold water
Oil for deep-frying
1 egg white, slightly beaten
1/4 to 1/2 cup finely chopped blanched
    pistachio nuts
Sifted confectioners' sugar

1. To make filling, beat cheese with vanilla extract. Add 1/2 cup confectioners' sugar and beat until smooth. Fold in candied citron and chocolate chips. Chill thoroughly.

2. To make shells, combine flour, sugar, cinnamon, and salt. Using a pastry blender, cut in shortening until pieces are the size of small peas. Stir in eggs, blend in vinegar and cold water.

3. Turn dough onto a lightly floured surface and knead until smooth and elastic (5 to 10 minutes). Wrap in waxed paper and chill 30 minutes.

4. Fill a deep saucepan a little over half full with oil. Heat oil slowly to 360° F.

5. Roll out chilled dough 1/8 inch thick. Using a 6 x 4 1/2-inch oval pattern cut from cardboard, cut ovals from dough with a pastry cutter or sharp knife.

6. Wrap dough loosely around cannoli tubes (see Note), just lapping over opposite edge. Brush overlapping edges with egg white and press together to seal.

7. Fry shells in hot oil about 8 minutes, or until golden brown, turning occasionally. Fry only a few at a time, being careful not to crowd them. Using a slotted spoon or tongs, remove from oil, and drain over pan before removing to paper towels. Cool slightly and remove tubes. Cool completely.

8. When ready to serve, fill shells with ricotta filling. Sprinkle ends of filled shells with pistachio nuts and dust shells generously with confectioners' sugar.

About 16 filled rolls

Note: Aluminum cannoli tubes or clean, unpainted wooden sticks, 6 inches long and 3/4 inch in diameter, may be used.

Strufoli

1 3/4 to 2 cups flour
1/4 teaspoon salt
3 eggs
1/2 teaspoon vanilla extract
1 cup honey

1 tablespoon sugar
2 tablespoons grated orange peel (optional)
Oil for deep-frying
1 tablespoon tiny multicolored candies

1. Put 1 cup flour and salt into a medium bowl. Make a well in center and add 1 egg at a time, mixing slightly after each addition. Add vanilla extract. Stir in more of the flour to make a soft dough.

2. Turn dough onto a floured surface and knead until dough is smooth and elastic. Cover and let stand about 30 minutes.

3. Divide dough into halves. Lightly roll each half into a rectangle 1/4-inch thick, cut into strips 1/4-inch wide. Use palm of hand to roll strips to pencil thickness. Cut into pieces about 1/4- to 1/2-inch long.

4. Fill a deep saucepan a little over half full with oil; heat slowly to 375 °F.

5. Put honey and sugar into a small (3-cup) skillet; place over low heat about 5 minutes. Stir in orange peel. Set aside but keep warm.

6. Add only as many pieces of dough at a time to hot oil as will float one layer deep. Fry 3 to 5 minutes, or until lightly browned, turning as necessary. Drain on paper towels.

7. Add hot cooked pieces to warm honey, stir until they are coated with syrup, then lift out with a slotted spoon or fork and put on a foil-covered tray.

8. Refrigerate until slightly chilled. Arrange in a conical shape on a serving plate: Invert a small custard cup at center of plate and pile the coated pieces over and around it. Sprinkle the tiny candies over the top.

9. To serve, spoon apart in clusters.

8 to 10 servings

Almond macaroons

1 can (8 ounces) almond paste, cut in pieces
1 cup plus 2 tablespoons sugar
2 egg whites
Pine nuts

1. Combine almond paste, sugar, and egg whites in a bowl and work with a spoon until smooth.
2. Drop by teaspoonfuls onto cookie sheets lined with unglazed paper. Top with pine nuts.
3. Bake at 325 °F. about 12 minutes, or until delicately browned. Cool slightly, then remove cookies to racks to cool.

About 3 dozen cookies

Festive decorations

Stained-glass window

1. Trace pattern onto **lightweight paper**. Rub back side of pattern with a **white drawing pencil** or **chalk**. Then, fold in half a sheet of **black construction paper** or similar paper. Position the traced pattern over the folded sheet with the pattern beginning at the edge of the fold and trace over the pattern again, using sufficient pressure to leave a white pattern line on top of the folded black sheet.

2. **Tape** the folded sheet to a cutting surface. Using a small **hobby knife**, cut out the areas that represent the different panes of stained-glass, making sure to cut through both layers of black construction paper at the same time. Do not cut window's outer edges yet.

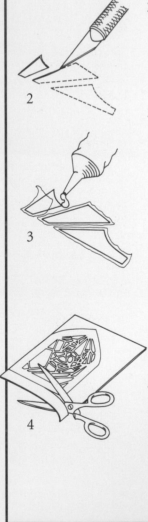

3. Following the color scheme, shown at right, use scissors to cut out pieces of **tissue paper** to fill the panes. To allow for gluing surface, make sure each piece is slightly larger than the area to be filled. Unfold the black sheet. Working at the inner surface of one window, use **glue** to attach the tissue pieces into place along the black lines that border each pane of stained glass.

Now glue the two halves of folded black paper together, applying glue lightly only to the black dividing lines and to the larger black areas around the edges. Do not spill glue on the tissue paper, through which the light will pass.

4. When the glue is dry, cut out the window itself. During the day, display the decoration in front of a sunny window. Otherwise, place in front of any available light source.

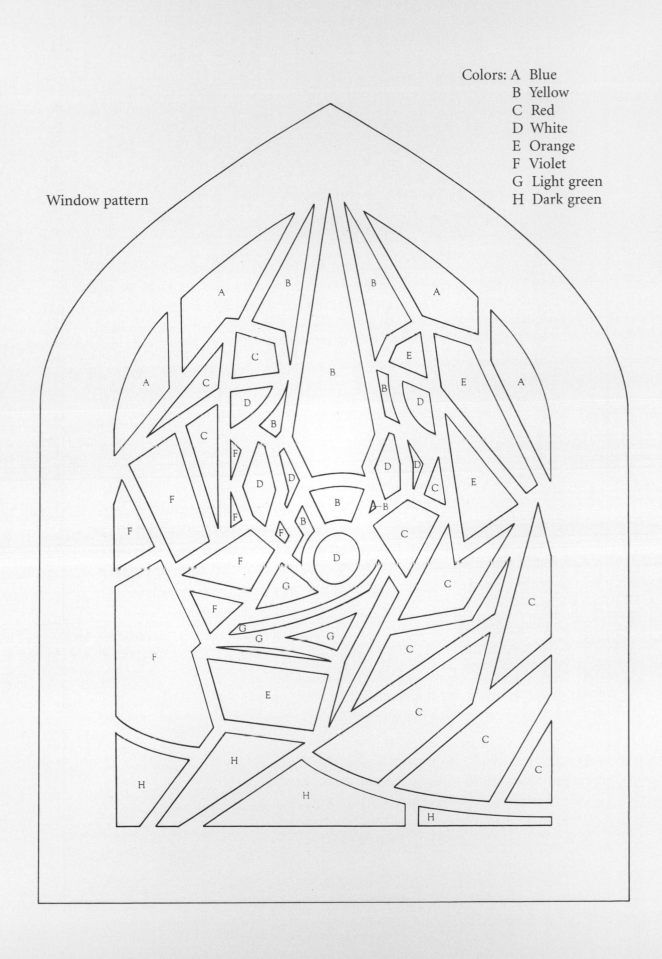

Window pattern

Colors: A Blue
        B Yellow
        C Red
        D White
        E Orange
        F Violet
        G Light green
        H Dark green

Quilled star

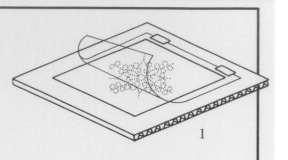

1. Trace complete design on **lightweight paper**. Lay paper pattern on a piece of **corrugated cardboard**. Tape a sheet of **wax paper** over pattern.

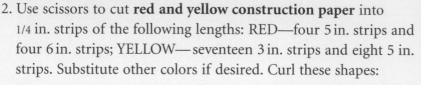

2. Use scissors to cut **red and yellow construction paper** into 1/4 in. strips of the following lengths: RED—four 5 in. strips and four 6 in. strips; YELLOW—seventeen 3 in. strips and eight 5 in. strips. Substitute other colors if desired. Curl these shapes:

   Tight Rolls Use eight 3 in. yellow strips. Moisten one end and, beginning with this end, roll the paper around the center of a **toothpick**. Keep paper tight as you roll. **Glue** loose end into place and hold until glue is dry. Carefully remove toothpick.

   Loose Roll Use one 3 in. yellow strip. Roll as for tight roll, then let roll unwind a bit. Glue loose end.

   Marquise Use four 6 in. red strips to make four loose rolls. Pinch each roll on either side to form an eye shape.

   Scroll Shapes Use eight 3 in. yellow strips. Loosely roll both ends of each strip towards the center, but not all the way to the center.

   "V" Shapes Use eight 5 in. yellow strips. Pinch each strip in the center, forming a *V*. Then roll ends loosely outward.

   Heart Shapes Use four 5 in. red strips. Pinch in center as for *"V"* shape, but roll ends inward to form a heart shape.

3. Arrange shapes, a few at a time, starting in the center and working out on wax paper over pattern.

4. With a toothpick, apply a dab of glue at each connecting point. While glue dries, anchor shapes with **stick pins** wherever necessary to bend and hold shapes in place. Remove pins when glue is completely dry. For hanging, attach looped **thread**.

Christmas songs

Carol of the Bagpipers

Traditional Sicilian
Translation: Dr. Theodore Baker, 1904

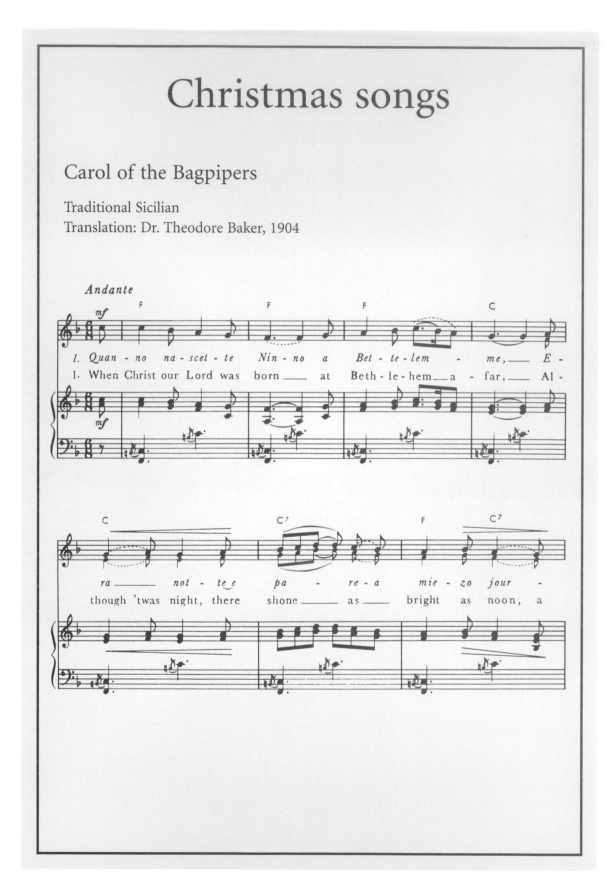

Walter Ehret, George K. Evans, *The International Book of Christmas Carols*,
© 1963, pp 242–250. Reprinted by permission.

From Starry Skies Thou Comest

Alphonsus Liguori (1696-1787)

2. *A te, che sei del mondo*
   Il creatore,
   Mancano panni e fuoco,
   O mio Signore.
   Caro, eletto pargoletto,
   Quanto questa poverta
   Piu m'innamora,
   Giacche ti fece amor povero
   ancora.

2. In Heav'n Thou wert Creator,
   The True and Only Word.
   Yet here on earth no fire, Lord,
   To keep Thee from the cold.
   Jesus, dearest little baby,
   Come in direst poverty,
   Would I had gifts for Thee!
   How wonderful God's love that
   suffers here for me!

Walter Ehret, George K. Evans, *The International Book of Christmas Carols*, © 1963, pp 242–250. Reprinted by permission.

Illustration acknowledgments

Cover: (front) © John Turner, Corbis, (back) © Brian Lawrence, SuperStock

2: © Nocenti/Olympia/Sipa

7: © Christine Webb, Alamy

9-10: AP/Wide World

13: © John Heseltine, Worldwide Picture Library/Alamy

14: © AFP/Getty Images

15: © Time Life Pictures/Getty Images

17: © 4Corners Images

19: © Bluered/Viesti Associates

20: © Michael A. Vaccaro from Louis Mercier

22: © G. DeBevilacqua, Viesti Associates

23: © Bluered/Viesti Associates

25-26: World Book photo by Jadwiga Lopez

27: Painting by Nunzia Falco from Christian Children's Fund, Inc.

28: © Grazia Meri, Woodfin Camp, Inc.

29: © Viesti Associates

31: L'Italia

32: Marka Graphic Photos & Archivium

33-34: Gaetano Barone

35: World Book photo by Steve Hale

37: © AFP/Getty Images

38: *St. Francis of Assisi Preparing the Christmas Crib at Grecchio* (1297). Fresco by Giotto di Bondone, San Francesco, Upper Church, Assisi, Italy. (© Giraudon/Bridgeman Art Library)

40: © Giuseppe De Pietro

41: © Bluered/Viesti Associates

42: © Marcella Pedone

43: © Riccardo Lombardo, Viesti Associates

44: (left) © John G. Ross, (right) © Giuseppe De Pietro

45: © Michael A. Vaccaro from Louis Mercier

47: © Vittorugo Contino

48-49: © Sandro Vannini, Corbis

50: (top) © David Lees, Corbis, (bottom) © Michael A. Vaccaro from Louis Mercier

51: © Grazia Meri, Woodfin Camp, Inc.

53: Bob Scott Studio Inc.

54: © gkphotography/Alamy

55: © Marcella Pedone

56: (top) World Book photo by Jadwiga Lopez, (bottom) Bernard Arendt

57: © Grazia Meri, Woodfin Camp, Inc.

59: © AFP/Getty Images

60: AP/Wide World

61: © AFP/Getty Images

62: © Livio Anticoli, Getty Images

63: © Reuters

64: © Michael A. Vaccaro from Louis Mercier

Advent Calendar: © 4Corners Images

Advent calendar art: Eileen Mueller Neill*

Recipe cards: Eileen Mueller Neill*

Craft Illustrations: Kathy Clo*

All entries marked with an asterisk (*) denote illustrations created exclusively for World Book, Inc.